Herald Ex

Pub W

in th

South Hams

Brian Carter

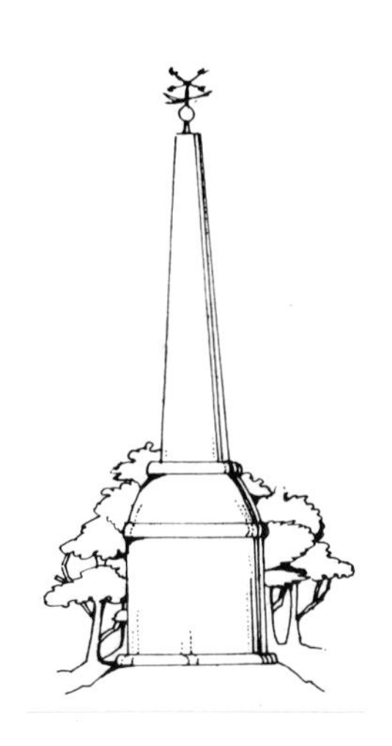

OBELISK PUBLICATIONS

Also by the Author

Walking "With a Tired Terrier" In and Around Torbay

Walks in the South Hams

Some Other 'Walks' Books

Diary of a Dartmoor Walker, *Chips Barber*

Diary of a Devonshire Walker, *Chips Barber*

Ten Family Walks on Dartmoor, *Sally & Chips Barber*

Ten Family Walks in East Devon, *Sally & Chips Barber*

The Templer Way, *Derek Beavis*

Walks in the Shadow of Dartmoor, *Denis McCallum*

Walks in Tamar and Tavy Country, *Denis McCallum*

Walks in the Totnes Countryside, *Bob Mann*

Walks in Chagford Country, *Terry Bound*

The Great Walks of Dartmoor, *Terry Bound*

Wheelchair Walks in Devon, *Lucinda Gardner*

For further details of these or any of our titles, please send an SAE to Obelisk Publications at the address below, or telephone (01392) 468556

Acknowledgements

All maps and drawings by Brian Carter

All photographs by Chips Barber

apart from pages 4 and 14 (top and bottom right)

Eight Devon Character Drawings (some in this book) are available as postcards from the Herald Express, Hamsworth House, Barton Hill Road, Torquay TQ2 8JN, Price £1 per set

First published in 1995 by

Obelisk Publications, 2 Church Hill, Pinhoe, Exeter, Devon

Designed by Chips and Sally Barber

Typeset by Sally Barber

Printed in Great Britain by

The Devonshire Press Limited, Torquay, Devon

Introduction

The South Hams is a magic corner of Britain. Here the towns are small and the countryside is big without being spectacular or intimidating. Leaving conurbation Torbay behind you can cross the Dart into a pastoral world that would have brought Bisto Kid smiles to my grandparents' faces. Everything is on a human scale, from the architecture in town and village to the landscape of coombes, low hills, copses, small fields and a coastline of extraordinary beauty.

The pubs match up to the scenery, from the red soil locals on the shores of Start Bay to the tucked-away inns pickled in history, either off or on the tourist trails. And their fayre varies from traditional pasties, cider and real ale, to more complicated cuisine, wine and perhaps an unusual malt whisky.

'A drap of Debn zider, ma boodies?'

This isn't a book for gungho backpackers out to clock up the miles in bleak hill country. The walks range from a modest two mile lane stroll to a ten mile coast and country hike. Lanes and coastal paths, often in secluded corners of the South Hams, provide access to some of the area's less familiar history and natural history.

Setting off from a pub car park you can explore leys, creeks, raised beaches, hamlets, hills, wild shores or quiet stretches of farmland. For companions you'll have wind, rain and sun, farm stock and the wildlife of one of Britain's loveliest backwaters.

These inn outings are for loners, couples, families or small groups of friends. Personally, my love affair with the South Hams has lasted a lifetime and I remain a self-confessed rural romantic, a walker in the tradition of Hazlitt, Borrow and Edward Thomas. For me a sunset and a pub fire have a lot in common, and the muddy lane leading out of the hills into Beesands has as much romance as the Road to Samarkhand.

A Devonian, I revel in the rural quality of my county, from the small print of the hedgerow to the sort of visions sky, sea and land can conjure up from a South Hams morning. But apart from the views and the pub fires I enjoy the actual business of walking – soaking up all the countryside has to offer.

There are seven walks, one for each day of the week and hopefully they'll give you a chance to share my passion for Nature, my homeland, oggies, cider, ale and old inns. The tavern treks take you from East Prawle, Beesands, South Pool and Slapton Leys to Frogmore, Ermington and Stokenham.

En route you'll meet a crop of winter lambs, free range Jack Russells, grazing Canada geese, goldfinches on thistle heads, scrounging Aylesbury ducks, calves, cows and pigs. Back in the bar you can sip a good farmhouse cider, enjoy a glass of ale, see off a Devon pasty or work your way at a leisurely pace through a lunch or an à la carte evening meal.

I like to think we can wander through a South Hams autumn and winter in the tradition of yesterday's wayfarers. So why not join me on the hills, in the coombes and by the fireside?

— 1 —

Travels Around the Globe

From the Globe Inn, Frogmore

(Keynedon, Sherford, Sherford Down Cross, Furze Cross and Frogmore again — five miles)

Frogmore is a village on the A379, almost halfway between Kingsbridge and Stokenham. If you park in the pub car park, please remember to inform the landlord of the Globe Inn of your intentions.

HANGING above the front door of the inn was an iridescent globe and the dimly lit bar was full of promise if you're hooked on log fires.

The early afternoon was having a bad attack of wind as I left the Globe Inn's car park and came along the busy A379 Kingsbridge–Torcross Road, through the village of Frogmore.

Cottages dozed, bungalow gardens waited for spring, Frogmore Bakery breathed a little warmth into the gale and I walked past the bridge and the modern development of Apple Tree Close to bear left again this time into a muddy lane signposted Sherford—13th Century Church, Cyder Press and Trout Farm. But this was by no means a Tourist Trail.

Frogmore

Presently, I was above small fields, a brook and lots of wild hedges. The wind roared, hissed and rumbled. Undergrowth and trees responded irritably — twitching, rocking and rolling or just thrashing about like biblical prophets tormented by fleas.

At the wayside Keynedon Farm was a grand old place with the air of a Domesday manor in aspic. Glass panels glowed from the gloom of the big front door arch and the stonework of the house and outbuildings was mellow grey. As working farms go it was very impressive and spooky, but a bit further up the lane I was reminded of a perennial problem of the age we live in.

The notice high on a wall of the next group of buildings read: Slow, please. Children and animals.

To speed in these lanes would be both crazy and criminal but some motorists obviously do, and I could imagine the impact a road hog would have on Keynedon Barton and Keynedon Mill. The mill is another relic of yesterday, but the pink house is very much lived in, although its isolation might not appeal to some people looking for a home in the country.

Beyond Keynedon the lane climbed to a gateway view of a coombe, an ancient linhay, a stream, meadows, a copse and more wild hedges rioting in the wind. From the hilltop I looked down on Sherford's roofs and church tower before walking the narrows between mossy walls into the hamlet.

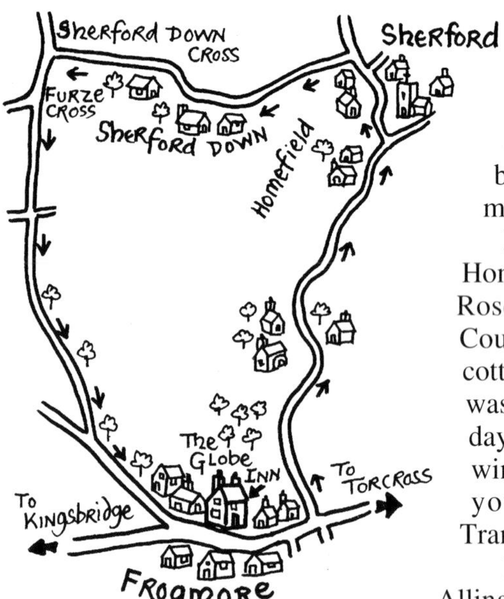

Beyond Old Homefield and Higher Homefield, the cream cottage called Rosebank, Martin's Court, gabled Court Hayes and some little little cottages, stood St Martin's Church. It was idyllic, even on a rough winter's day with mud everywhere and the wind as melodramatic as anything you'd expect to find on a Transylvanian Walking Tour.

My route was signposted East Allington 3, while a smaller sign nearby read: Stancombe Cider. The road ran between more small cottages with roofed doors and the odd thatched roof or thatched porch. A Jack Russell crossed my path and a second ran downhill, followed by a third at a leisurely pace. Close at hand someone was calling them and I wondered if their walkabouts were part of a DIY exercise routine.

Sherford ended with more ancient cottages up a side lane, barns, a footpath, Rose Cottage, Mount Pleasant and, after I had swung left at the crossroads to take the Charleton trail, a flourish of council houses.

Red mud and wayside sycamores saw me to Sherford Down Farm with its barns, byres, muck and straw. These credentials of rural authenticity only needed the ghost of my gran feeding the chickens to complete the scene.

At Sherford Down Cross it was left once more, which is inevitable, I suppose, considering the geography of the circuit I was walking. But along the road at Furze Cross it was straight on up a really muddy lane that narrowed on its roller coaster run to give me a hilltop view of the creek and the estuary before I came down the backway into Frogmore again. Then I cleaned my boots and headed for the Globe.

The early nineteenth century pub waited at the roadside and through the door and out of the wind the atmosphere was as warm as the big log fire burning in the bar where pictures of seascapes and nautical scenes hung on the walls. The ceilings were low, the chairs and settles comfortable and an upright piano stood in the corner. Innkeepers Duncan and Sheila Johnston smiled their welcomes.

Every table had its candle in a bottle and vase of flowers and people were waiting for their desserts at the end of what must have been good lunches judging by their comments.

At the top end of the bar was the à la carte restaurant and its soft, orange lighting. More candles in bottles stood on the tables, and the settee and armchairs in the corner were a nice, homely touch. As far as ambience goes it was a happy cross between barn and cottage sitting room. With time due to be called in twenty minutes I was too late for food, but a glass of Murphy's was all I needed after a large, late breakfast. Sharing the fireside with my old Irish friend, Murphy, was

Frogmore Creek

satisfactory. Outside, the blustery afternoon threatened rain, but the pub fire, cheerful service and that laid-back atmosphere was a good way bring another South Hams happening to a close.

— 2 —

Fine Weather for Ducks on the Trail of the Mill Brook

From the Millbrook Inn, South Pool

(South Pool, Lee Lane End, Loo Cross, Ford, Chivelstone, Herring Street and South Pool again, 6 miles)

From Kingsbridge take the A379 Torcross road and turn right at Frogmore over the bridge, signposted South Pool. Park carefully and thoughtfully near the pub.

THE morning was damp and misty after heavy rain when I arrived in South Pool, a hamlet on one of the prettiest creeks of the Kingsbridge Estuary. The spring tide had covered the stepping stones at the ford and the Millbrook Inn's celebrated Aylesbury ducks were quietly quacking as I set off uphill, comforted by the lights in the bar windows.

Passing old mossy stone walls and cottages with roofed doors I came to the turning that led to the thirteenth century church of St Nicholas and St Cyriac. Then the single track road squeezed between banks hackled with bare trees. But if I'd wanted a breather I could have sat on the community bench and looked down on South Pool from a patch of grass where the green lane descent to the creek begins.

On the brow of the hill were the outbuildings and tractors of a working farm, and the faint smell of the wet countryside was spiced with the stink of slurry. Rainsoaked farmland rolled gently away into vague distances and I came downhill to Long Cross and straight on to Lee Lane Cross where the route was signposted Molescombe and Chillington.

Even on a grey, misty November day the South Hams countryside had a haunting beauty and it was nice to be on the sort of route that isn't normally used by hikers or ramblers. The lane was narrow, muddy and puddly. It carried me past Molescombe Farm on the bend to the junction where Molescombe House was signposted. Sheep were motionless in fields blurred by fine rain, with the rest of the South Hams lost in the haze of bad weather.

At Loo Cross I turned sharp right and wandered up the hill towards an amazing light in the sky. The morning was marvellously alive in the silence of the naked trees, or trees down to their last few leaves, in the far off cawing of rooks and the hedgerow flutter of a robin.

At Marber Cross the signpost sent me on towards Kernborough and Ford. But the flail-mowed hedges didn't seem necessary, even though they opened up another soft sweep of farmland where the lane suddenly dipped and wound on, up and down, into the rain murk of a landscape edited by autumn.

Houses were few, and literally far between, and the solitude had a friendly texture, helped by a couple of dishevelled little ponies gazing at me through a five-barred gate as I swung past the Kernborough sign. And I'm not taking liberties with the truth when I confess that my happiness fed on the way the lonely country road brought me into contact with just a few birds and farm animals. Light gleamed on mud, cow dung and rain water as I made the long descent into the tiny hamlet of Ford. Mill House waited at Ford Cross and I came straight on, trusting in the arm of the signpost which read: East Prawle and East Portlemouth.

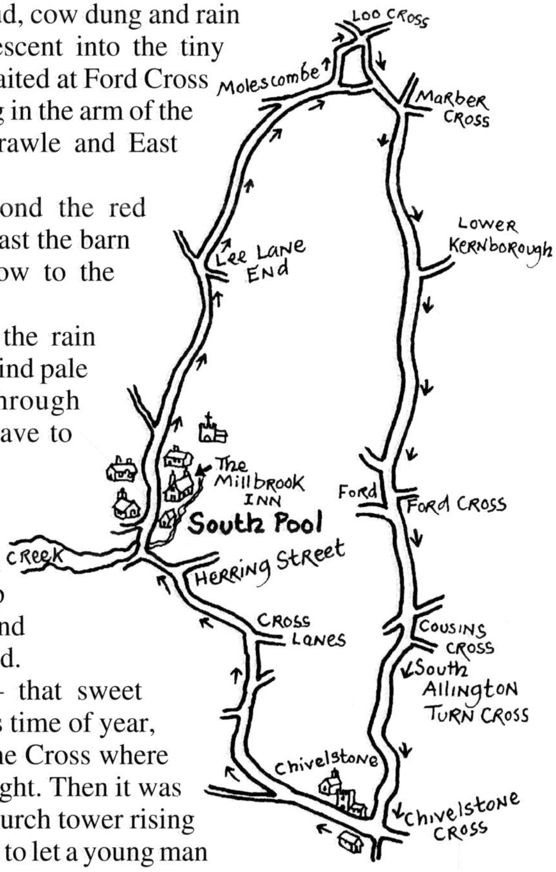

Then I was climbing beyond the red telephone box on the corner past the barn conversions of Brook Meadow to the hilltop and Cousin's Cross.

Here, for no reason at all the rain stopped and the sun shone behind pale grey cloud, like a lamp through curtains. Yet again I didn't have to bear left or right. All I had to do was point myself in the direction of South Allington Turn Cross, ignore the South Allington sign and just keep going, up and down, and round about, along the two track road.

A robin burst into song – that sweet meditative song it sings at this time of year, and I walked on to Chivelstone Cross where Chivelstone was signposted right. Then it was fine to be greeted by a grey church tower rising above cottage roofs, and pause to let a young man and his dog see a herd of South Devons safely on their way from the milking shed.

Chivelstone is an isolated community of old houses, a farm full of life and little conceded to the developer-dominated carve-up of rural Devon. Inevitably, a muddy lane brought me to a fork and a right-hand turn into an even muddier lane with many twists and turns above a great wooded coombe with the creek in the distance.

Eventually the switchback saw me to another South Hams hilltop and another descent, this time to Cross Lanes where South Pool was signposted left. Here many of the features I associate with this part of Devon were orchestrated – a copse on a distant ridge, sheep in a pasture, rain water running through the mud of a secret lane, the absence of grandeur and the spectacular; in other words, homely countryside and everything on a human scale, yet uncluttered by houses.

Hands in pockets I walked down to Herring Street Cross and on into South Pool past Rosemary's Cottage, Farthingfield and South Pool Church Hall, to the ford at South Pool Cross. Then it was right over the bridge for a close-up of Devon pink cottages and weather-worn thatch on the final few yards to the Millbrook Inn once more.

In the really pubby little back bar, where nothing has been updated, I found Jeremy Spedding preparing for the lunchtime trade. Jeremy and his partner, Liz Stirland, took over from his mum and dad, Cindy and Arthur Spedding.

Looking out the window I saw five of the normally nine strong Aylesbury contingent preening muddy feathers on the far side of the Mill Brook, the stream which gave the pub its name and flows beside the beer terrace.

This terrace, facing the brook and the duck cabaret, plus the Millbrook's reputation for good food, has made the pub a popular haunt for people from Plymouth to Torbay.

As pubs go it's a gem – from the Aylesburies and ale to the cider and cottage pie, the low ceilings and friendly atmosphere. It certainly put a pleasant fullstop to the sort of laze along a lane that deserves the label – memorable.

— 3 —

The Pig Connection

From the Pig's Nose Inn, East Prawle

(Higher House Farm, Chivelstone Cross, South Allington, Lannacombe Green Cross, Lannacombe Beach and the coastal path to Prawle Point. Then the bridle path to East Prawle again—ten miles)

From Kingsbridge take the A379 to Frogmore, turn right over Frogmore Bridge and then follow the narrow country road to East Prawle via Lee Lane End Cross, Ford Cross, Cousins Cross, Chivelstone Cross and Knowle Fork.

A SOLITARY dog violet was in bloom against the wall of Piglet Stores and Grunter's Cafe beside the small car park opposite the Pig's Nose Inn.

It was another reminder of the mild autumn — but why all the porker references, my dear Watson? Well, that would be revealed ten miles later.

I was hungry for some brisk exercise at the sort of pace that makes me aware of old leg muscles. So off I went on one of those wild mornings of swift, heavy showers, with sunlight and cloud shadows flying.

East Prawle is small. Less than 150 people live in the hilltop hamlet which overlooks the Channel. The environment is incredibly beautiful and each season has its peaks.

'You'm like my old man on the bliddy scrumpy'

I walked past a row of old cottages, the Providence Inn and a farm into countryside soaked in sunlight and rain. The sign on the verge by a pond and some young willows, read: Caution, Ducks Crossing. Maybe there was a link between that splash of wetland and the little school up the road, a building which is now a study centre.

Calves gazed at me from the pen over the way and caulies and swedes were on sale at the entrance to a farm, which according to the stone pillar at the entrance, was called ER... OU .. E .. AR. About to rejoice in this bit of Devon dialect gibberish I saw the real name which time and the weather hadn't tampered with. It read: Higher House Farm.

The wind gusted to gale force. Country smells whirlpooled and a great vista of South Hams farmland opened before me. Low hills, green fields, the occasional scattering of houses, a wood and the far off lights of Salcombe over the water made a landscape no true lane walker could resist.

Just before Chivelstone Cross I took a right hand turn down the narrow lane signed Lannacombe, past little fields divided by drystone walls, two rows of old cottages with roofed doors, and an old country house, into one of those tucked away coombes which travellers seldom visit. Sheep grazed in cider apple orchards and I came on through the tiny community of South Allington to South Allington Cross where my way was once again marked Lannacombe.

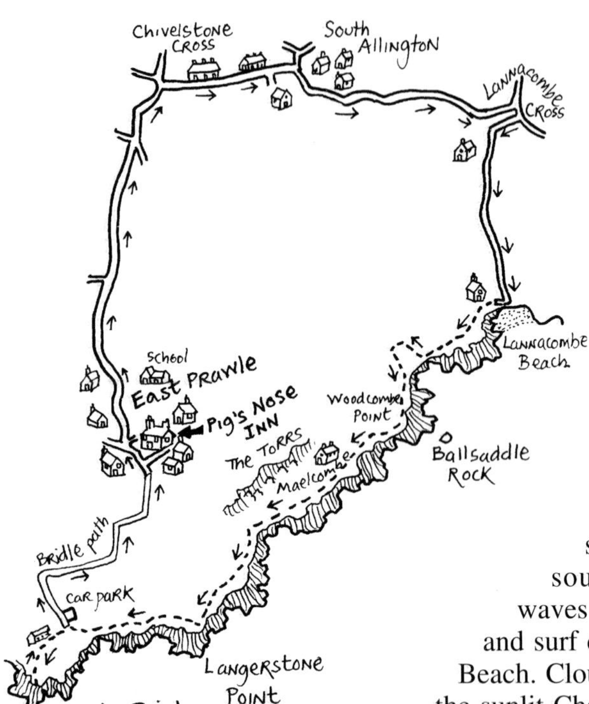

It was great to plod uphill with the gleam of red plough on the left, between tall hedges, in the roar of the wind, and air that sparkled.

Right at Lannacombe Cross brought me almost immediately to another sharp right turning to Lannacombe, and I walked the long muddy cart track under hillsides of gorse and thorn, through the marshy coombe and its willows to the sea. And what a sea! In the teeth of the south-easterly gale great waves thundered over the rocks and surf creamed up Lannacombe Beach. Cloud shadows swept across the sunlit Channel as I swung right at Lannacombe Cottage and came through the surf roar onto one of the most beautiful stretches of coastal path in Britain.

The contrast between the lanes and farmland I had left behind couldn't have been greater. Walking through the blackthorn thickets I met the full force of the gale. A drench of spray fizzled around me and I came through the gap in the wall onto the tip of Woodcombe Point where the sea gleamed under a sky dark in places with falling showers and sunbright in others.

The path ran on below jagged outcrops poking from the hillsides, pinnacles and rock towers, past Ballsaddle Rock and Stinking Cove, into salt spray and surf thunder to the meadow that sloped gently to Maelcombe House which was set back against pines and bare ash.

The distinctive rocks on the hill above Maelcombe Point were called The Torrs

Lannacombe

— the Gaelic equivalent of our Dartmoor tors.

Crossing the next meadow to the low crags on the edge of the shore I walked pastures bounded by drystone walls or wild hedges towards the rock towers of Langerstone Point. Every now and then the path strayed as close as possible to the top of the low shoreline cliffs where spray was rising like drizzle. I didn't mind a wet head, though. It was Emily Brontë weather.

Surf boiled around rocks and mussel reefs, seabirds shot inland, a couple of crows tried unsuccessfully to beat into the wind and Prawle Point waited in the bottom of the sky. A few more meadows and I was beyond the 1939-45 War bunkers, sharing the final grassy hillside with a handful of ewes and their lambs.

Moments later I was on top of Prawle leaning against the wind beside the deserted Coastguard Station. The views both north and south were remarkable.

Northward were the crags and headlands I had just passed to reach this dominating coastal feature. To the south sunlight lay on the bar where Salcombe estuary met the sea and the land ended at the great crags of Bolt Head.

Here everything was vast — sea, sky, the sweep of countryside. But retracing my steps down the field past the row of Coastguard cottages I found one of the smallest lambs I've ever seen and the beauty of life in that creature was the counterpoint of the landscape's grandeur.

Over the stile I came left to another stile and the car park. Then the rough lane, which is a bridleway, took me up on the long haul through a right and a left turning, both of which were signposted East Prawle, to the windswept huddle of houses on the hilltop.

Ben Newport had just opened the front door of the Pig's Nose Inn and leaving my muddy boots in the porch I went in in my socks to warm my hands in front of the fire.

East Prawle

Ben and his wife, Ann, have been at the pub for many years, and if the bar is like home from home, with its settee and arm chair, it's because, after hours, it's the Newport's sitting room.

Here you can get a game of darts, chat about the birdlife of Prawle Point or simply find a table and enjoy a meal and a pint.

But something on the extensive menu instantly caught my eye — a Devon

Former Lloyd's Signal Station on Prawle Point

Village scene at East Prawle

pasty. Well, being red soil born and bred how could I resist an oggie from the holy side of the Tamar?

Whilst I sipped the coffee I browsed around the pig pictures and pig memorabilia on the bar room walls.

Then the name of the pub and other East Prawle porker connections like the Piglet Stores and Grunter's Cafe outside became clear.

The inn is about 500 years old.

"It was the Union Hotel, then the Union Inn till 1949, when it was rechristened The Pig's Nose," Ann said.

"After the Pig's Nose Rock near Gammon Head and the Ham Stone." Ben smiled.

"Francis Bacon didn't sleep here, did he?" I asked.

'They'm prime tetty oggies, me 'ansome.'

Pigs apart, if you're new to the county and wonder why Devon has 'Glorious' parked permanently in front of it, pay a visit to Prawle Point on a wild December morning.

View from Prawle Point towards Lannacombe

— 4 —

Favourite Places in a Favourite Place

From the Cricket Inn, Beesands

(Beesands, Tinsey Head, Hallsands, Batton, Huckham and Beesands again – 4 miles)

Take the A379 Torcross road from Kingsbridge. At the Stokenham roundabout turn right for Start Point. The narrow lane to Beeson and Beesands is signposted on the left. Widdicombe Ley is left (north) along the shore.

YOU can no more judge a walk by its length than food by the amount heaped on your plate. Well, when I arrived at Beesands, a fishing hamlet strung out above the shingle and pebble banks of Start Bay, I wasn't in the mood to clock up the miles. I wanted a modest workout, garnished with the sort of beauty the sea, sky and hilly farmland can conjure up – given the right light.

The autumn cloud-drift was low, a buzzard flapped off, mobbed by gulls, and the sun shone on Start Bay. The first smoke of morning crept from chimneys and a shoulder of fox-coloured bracken was hunched against the clouds above the hamlet.

Beesands before the new protective sea wall

The sea views were spectacular and although the Cricket Inn was closed I knew it would be open when I returned. Timing is the essence of this sort of walk. It's no use sniffing around a warm looking pub only to find its doors shut at the end of the walk when your need for food, fireside and a little booze has peaked to a pleasant plateau of anticipation.

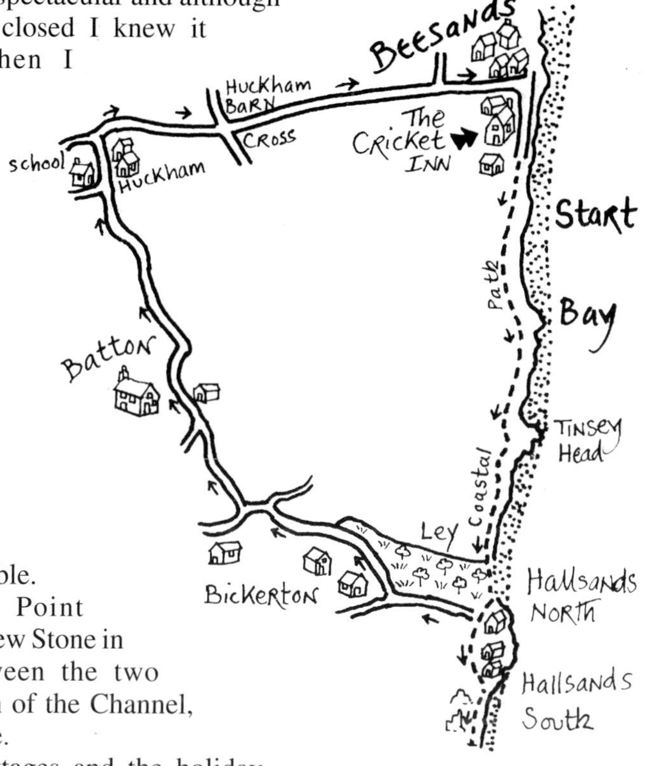

But the sea views can't be consigned to the margins of this walk. They're remarkable. Southward is Start Point lighthouse, with the Mew Stone in the North, and between the two sprawls a great stretch of the Channel, with a knifeblade glare.

The fishermen's cottages and the holiday

The North Hallsands Hotel

homes are mostly small, with porches and little windows. Facing the sea they know what it's like to be mugged by storms which roar in on a mighty flexing of marine muscle to sweep communities like Beesands into the headlines.

Dinghies were parked among cars on the seafront and the row of cottages led me to the coastal path which was signposted Hallsands. It ran above the rooftops with sunlight shafting between clouds and the lighthouse standing in the bottom of the sky.

The path is narrow and can be muddy where it follows the clifftop. Big flocks of woodpigeons passed over my head as the hamlet of Hallsands North came into sight and the giant radio masts on the hill were half lost in sun haze.

Presently the slop track dumped me on Hallsands beach, below a large bed of reeds and osiers which was once a ley like the freshwater lagoons at Slapton. The shingle is dotted with signs warning walkers of 'sharp objects on the beach' presumably washed in from the submerged, off-shore wreck. Overlooking the scene, from a bluff on the hillside, is the Hallsands Hotel. I came up the path behind it to some holiday apartments and a summer tea room.

Ruins of Hallsands Village

Here the way dropped to the tiny abandoned fishing community of Hallsands South. The cottages were destroyed in the Great Storms of 1917 and, despite the Devon County Council notice which told me the road was liable to subsidence, I went and had a look at the ruins. Sadly, all that remains of Hallsands South is a chimney breast, the wall of a cottage, the shell of a building, a heap or two of stones, a touch of sea campion and an air of melancholy. If you've ever stood in one of those deserted Hebridean crofting communities, killed off by the Clearances, you'll know the feeling.

Retracing my steps to the beach I met the growl of a tractor beneath more flights of woodpigeon and the hedge-hugging swoops of chaffinch flocks. All that life in the sky was comforting and I felt OK about leaving the coast at the little car park below the Hallsands Hotel and taking to the lanes. Contrast can contribute to the quality of a walk. So, with the wind hissing through the reeds of the choked ley, I strolled past the small houses and bungalows of Bickerton to find my route signposted Kingsbridge.

Puddles, sunlight, mud most of the way beside the reeds, a pair of crows sailing overhead in such obvious enjoyment of each other's company that I had to smile – the rural cameos were as varied as they were familiar. But I wasn't looking for novelty. Nature and the seasons are all about recycling, from the first primrose of winter and the last leaf on the tree to our response to what's on offer. OK, there's nothing new about what a litre of my favourite vintage cider or a kiss from my little grand-daughter can give me, but in many respects familiarity brews its own magic.

Up the hill, ignoring the turning to Middlecombe Farm, I swung right at the smallholding and came along a track, with grass in the middle, to another junction.

"If you want Beesands", a woman said as she got in her car, "keep going right all the way to Huckham Barn Cross."

A moment or two later, while ambling through the centre of Batton Farm, I discovered the lady was Mrs Fraser, wife of the farmer who was chatting to his worker by the calf pen. The warmth of his Devon accent reminded me of my dad.

Mr Fraser showed me around.

"It's an old farm, buyh," he said, pointing to the beams in the barn. They had been 'rescued' from ships wrecked on Start Bay's rocks. The ladder leading to the loft came from an old sailing schooner and there were echoes of the past in the cider press.

But the hard reality of this part of the South Hams is the exodus of born and bred locals and the influx of incomers to the second homes, holiday homes and permanent retirement pads.

At the next crossroads my route was marked Huckham and here I found a small empty school, once the heart of the farming area and now the summer site of holiday visits by kids from Exmouth. Needless to say, it was with another jolt of heartache that I walked on past South Barn and Huccombe Farmhouse to bear right again at The Cottage. Then it was Huckham Barn Cross and a stiffish uphill slog before the reward of a buzzard-eye view of Beesands and Start Bay shimmering like a mackeral.

Down I came past the late bloom of wild flowers, boats stranded high and dry in gardens and the little white church of St Andrew to the seaside pub owned and run by Cyril Courtney and his wife, Maggie.

Cyril was born at the Cricket Inn in 1930 and the pub has been in the family since 1921, with Cyril at the helm since the late '60s. Doyen of Beesands soccer, he was a good all-round amateur sportsman, playing soccer, cricket, golf and squash until 'dicky' hips sidelined him. But he's still a keen angler.

I played against some of the great Beesands teams of the 1950s and they were by no means shy, polite encounters. In fact, no prisoners were taken and in those hard but happy days legend insisted that the Beesands team came straight off the crab boats, straight onto the pitch, with their football boots slung from their necks.

The main bar is more like auntie's parlour than the engine room of a busy tavern. There's a dart board, wooden panelling, coloured prints of characters from the pub's past, photographs of Cyril's gamekeeper grandad, the presence of other ancestors and a sense of the continuity of Beesand's life, both sides of the bar.

The Cricket Inn

Maggie doesn't serve elaborate meals but the crab in her sandwiches is local when it's available, and the pasties are among Dewdney's best. Seafood is obviously a feature. Maggie's food is tasty and Cyril is a cheerful Devonian with a sense of humour that puts me in mind of my dad. He keeps a good pint of draught Guinness, three real ales, Bass, and Churchward's farmhouse cider.

Well, I was ready for a snack, so I settled for a half of Churchward's Agricultural Wine, one of Mr Dewdney's oggies and a half dozen of Cyril's jokes.

Between lulls in the laughter I read one of the notices on his Noticeboard:

'Wanted – Woman to cook and clean fish, dig worms and make love. Must have good boat and motor. Please enclose picture of boat and motor.'

After a dose of sun, wind and salt air I was glad to find a pub full of human warmth there on the shores of Start Bay. I only wish my old Dad had been alive to contribute a few of his jokes to the lunchtime session.

— 5 —

See What I Saw Passing Marjery Cross

From the Crooked Spire Inn, Ermington

(Ermington, Marjery Cross, Todmore Cross, Westlake, Whipple's Cross and Ermington again; three rollercoaster miles)

Drive to Totnes in the Dartington direction. Then swing left for Kingsbridge at the traffic lights roundabout, come up the hill to the next set of traffic lights and it's right, along the B3210 Avonwick-Ugborough road. In Ermington there is free parking in the square in front of the Crooked Spire Inn.

THE Crooked Spire Inn gets its name from Ermington's church with the leaning spire. The village is the classic South Hams mix of houses, large and small, and cottages, with the Post Office Stores in the square across the road from the pub.

It was a wet morning after a rainy night but the weather was brightening as I set off for a brief village walkabout. If I had been playing this one by the book I would have started close to opening time for the usual bar snack lunch and a half of something interesting in a glass. But I fancied a breakfast-time stroll, after days and some nights with my nose to the grindstone.

The sky was covered in small, innocent-looking clouds and the surrounding hills were covered with small green fields and wild hedges. The churchyard on a slope was open to everything nature and the elements had to offer. But the church was locked so I wandered back to the inn with just the tinkle of a blackbird's winter song for company. Day had broken less than half an hour ago and a small boy was trotting home with the morning paper.

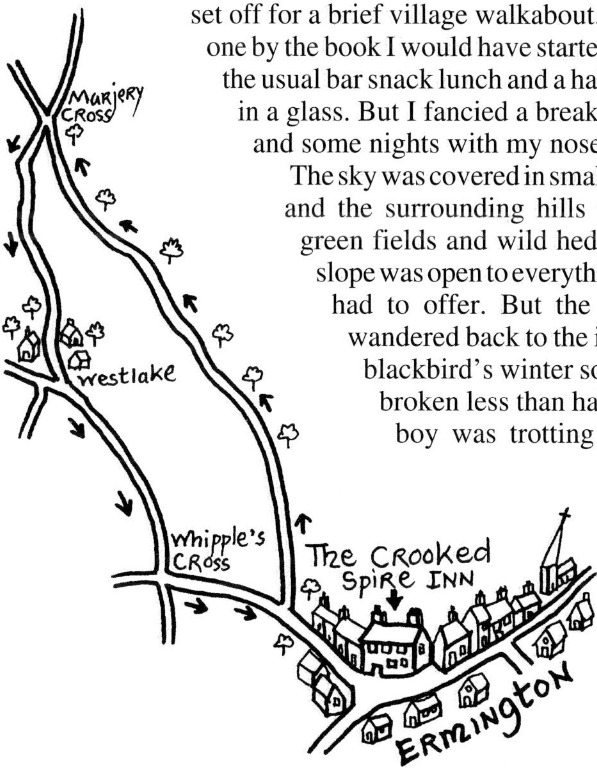

From the pub I went up the steep hill on the right past some cottages, the chapel, a row of little grey houses and the old phone box. Then at the crossroads I bore right again and the narrow lane led me into the countryside.

The high hedgebanks were crying out for primroses and the gaunt transmitter tower waited on the hilltop. Bare trees stood on bare hills and at the tower I stopped for the inevitable gateway view east. Pink and gold seams had appeared between clouds and Dartmoor's Henlake Down, Hanger Down and Butterdon Hill formed the Northern horizon.

The sun was up above the clouds now, and looking down I could see the sprawl of Ivybridge above the invisible A38. The clarity, after hours of heavy rain, was marvellous with distant features registering like holograms.

I didn't like the flail-shorn hedges, though, and no amount of beautiful sky could compensate for that sorry sight. But by winter wheat and glittering root crops I came straight over the crossroads, past more small fields to Marjery Cross for a very sharp turn left, signed Ermington.

Marching along I considered the delights of my lovely county. Beyond the relentless growth of conurbations, and their urban-fringe development, the farmland runs to moor and sea with most of the changes absorbed by the seasons. Or should I say absolved by the seasons?

A few scattered bungalows and houses later I was walking into the sun, to Todmore Cross, with Ermington signposted again. Pausing to blow my nose I thought a good name for this part of the way would be Sunrise Lane. But farm folk are more practical and it was probably Kracketty Lane (Kracketty is the old Devon dialect word for that little brown bird, the wren).

Indifferent to my progress the sun blazed from the hilltop ahead and I gave a cock pheasant a warm 'Good Morning' as it moved swiftly into the grass verge. My Dad would have saluted the bird with a clap of the shotgun and Mum would have applauded. But *horas non numero nisi serenas* is a reasonable motto, and the morning was too sunny to be thinking about bagging wildlife for the pot.

Then I was in the little community of Westlake, among a hotch potch of shacks, cottages, houses and a scrapyard. From Westlake Cross it was straight on, up the hill, under a vault of leafless branches, the way flanked by very tall hedgebanks. On the brow of the hill I met the full glare of the sun, a fiery disc there in the lower sky, and it was sunlit trees and meadows down to Whipple's Cross where the arm of the signpost pointing left read: Ermington, half a mile. Beyond, the lane dipped to reveal a broad landscape of those characteristically small fields, coombes and hills. A couple of cock pheasants strode among a group of crows and daws in a laneside field and I came out of a hollow and up towards Ermington's roofs and chimneys.

From the crossroads on the edge of the village I walked down to the pub behind a mother taking her two young sons to primary school.

Ermington's 'Crooked Spire'

By now I was having doubts about the early start, but Keith, partner of The Crooked Spire's landlady, Kathie Shopland, made me welcome despite being rushed off his feet making breakfast for the guests. Then I sipped my coffee by the stove in the bar and had a look round.

At the far end was the attractive restaurant, with its comfortable padded settles, and tables laid ready for the wining and dining. The bar was a real snug of a place reminiscent of some of the handsome little bars I've discovered on the west coast of Ireland.

Well, I've drunk at The Crooked Spire a couple of times in the past and found the hospitality matched the service. I only wish I hadn't arrived that morning like the telephone bill on the front door mat.

All you have to do to enjoy the Crooked Spire Inn, its bar, the glowing stove, or the restaurant, is arrive at a sociable time of day and don't push your luck like I did.

— 6 —

Nature's Small Print... and a Low Beam!

From the Tradesmans Arms, Stokenham

(Old Quarry Farm, Frittiscombe, Coleridge Cross, Carehouse Cross and Stokenham again – just under 2 miles)

Take the Kingsbridge road at Totnes. Come through Kingsbridge to the Quay and drive towards Torcross. The Tradesman's Arms is first left down from Carehouse Cross, Stokenham on the way to Torcross.

STOKENHAM is a quiet little community and I liked the Tradesman's Arms because it had that tucked away, friendly look about it. The roof is part-tiled, part-thatched, and the small inn stood among cottages, back from the A379, five miles from Kingsbridge.

It was nearly opening time on that grey morning. Surprisingly, the rain had stopped but as I left the pub car park and turned right I wondered if it was another of those cruel tricks the weather had been playing for weeks. Ninety per cent of fair starts had foul endings, or foul middles. But the church tower of fifteenth Century St Michael and All Angels was superimposed on a landscape of fields below hills and woods. If the view was a South Hams cliché I loved it. There must be scenes in heaven which the good spirits know almost as well as the bottoms of their cider glasses but I bet they still walk or fly towards them whistling.

'One lil sip woan 'urt'ee, ma flower.'

A few yards further on (I'm not into metres or kilometres) I bore left into a narrow, winding, uphill lane. The banks at either hand were tall and rocky, covered in ivy and ferns. A few scattered properties and I made a sharp right, followed by an equally sharp left, turn at the bungalow called Kiln Lodge. Then it was uphill again towards bare trees printed on clouds, past Old Quarry Farm, between high, flail-mowed hedges.

An old barn stood on the left, sheep were in a wayside field and small birds were in the hedge near the entrance to the drive that led to France Farm. The lane had a hard surface and the walking was easy.

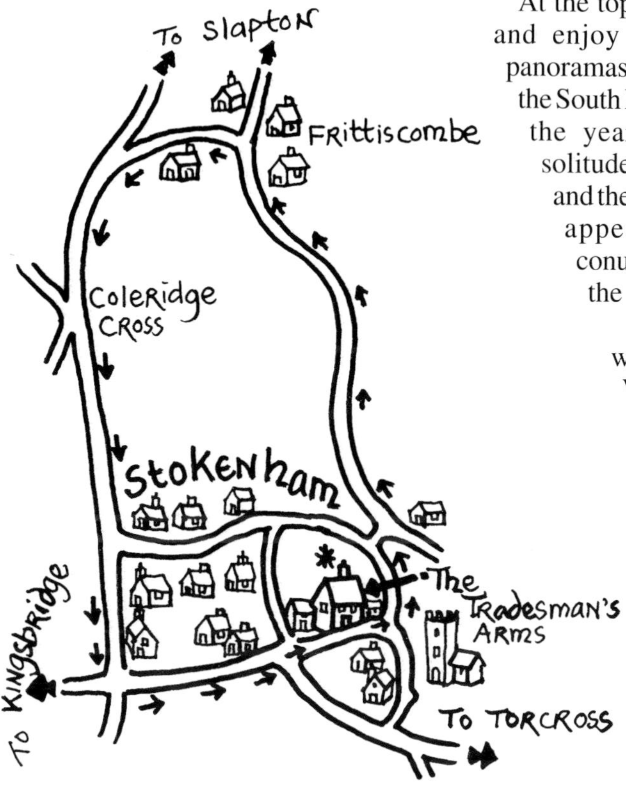

At the top of the hill I could stop and enjoy one of those typical panoramas of farmland which make the South Hams special throughout the year. All those acres of solitude, open to the weather and the seasons, are remarkably appealing if you are conurbation-stranded most of the time.

The walk continued with a steep descent. Water ran free on the left of the lane, while grass and mud occupied a band in the middle. Then I came round the corner to find an old farmhouse on the bend and a solitary brown hen skirting the flooded bottom. Calves stared at me through a gate and I was watched by a Jack Russell as I approached the big old house called Frittiscombe. The complex of buildings in the coombe was delightful, and the old weathered stonework, the stone walls and the remoteness of the place were enough to bring a Bisto Kid smile to the face of any true rural romantic.

At the Slapton–Stokenham Road I made another left turn and walking up the hill had the chance to read some of Nature's small print on the hedge banks. Harts tongue ferns at road level were a change from telegraph poles at sky level. But it wasn't long before I reached Coleridge Cross where Stokenham was signposted half a mile.

On another occasion, in a different mood I might have taken the public footpath over the winter wheat, but I was sticking to my lanes – puddles and all.

In keeping with the South Hams tradition, the high ground presented me with a splendid view of Start Bay and one of those winter get-togethers of sea and sky. Even the flail-mowed hedges couldn't diminish it.

The final leg was downward and on the hillside across the valley a field glinted red as if I needed a reminder that I was in Devon. A woman on a horse trotted by and we exchanged smiles before I came into Stokenham again past the village school and the bungalows to Carehouse Cross and the A379.

Bearing left I walked at a brisk pace along that short section of the busy Kingsbridge–Torcross Road for the turn off into Stokenham's quiet backwaters and the Tradesman's Arms once more.

Proprietor Peter Henderson had lit the log fire and was shooing Blanket, the pub's big white Italian sheepdog, back to its own quarters when I planted myself in the bar and looked around. The ceiling was low and so was the doorway as my head had discovered! The bar with the fire, wooden tables, chairs and beams had definite customer appeal. It was small and unpretentious, like the dining area which also boasted a log fire.

One of the most impressive things about the old pub is Peter's collection of malt whiskies, including a few Hebridean triumphs I've sampled on trips to the islands spanning several decades.

"The place has a lot of history," Peter said. "It dates back to 1390 and is mentioned in the local manorial roles as an ale house used by merchants walking the old bridle path with their pack mules."

The bar beckoned and he went to keep a customer happy while I moved to the side of the fire and my chilblains stopped jumping.

— 7 —

Wartime, Maritime – and Time for a Little Sea Food

from The Start Bay Inn, Torcross

(Along the Leys of Slapton to Strete Gate and back along the top of the shore above Start Bay – about five flat miles)

Take the Kingsbridge road out of Totnes and pick up the Torcross road, the A379 at the quay. Then drive until you reach the village. The tank carpark is down the road on the left, in the Strete Gate direction, just beyond the last houses of Torcross.

DRIZZLE swirled around me as I left the World War Two tank in the car park on the edge of Torcross, just down the road from the Start Bay Inn. Church bells rang, reeds hissed like swans and the water of the Lower Ley was dotted with wildfowl.

The tank is a monument to the hundreds of American servicemen who died in Start Bay in April 1944 when their ships were sunk by German E boats during a beach assault exercise for the Invasion of Europe.

Start Bay was across the road on my right and views of the nature reserve leys and the countryside beyond opened up to the left as I let the wind and rain sweep me towards distant Strete Gate. The narrow path ran above the reed beds, a swan made a noisy take off and there were goldfinches at the thistleheads. In fact, I've seen a lot of these little birds on my South Hams treks and they have the power to lift the spirit on the darkest day.

Another splash of gold came from the gorse in bloom. Willows rocked among the bramble thickets and watching the birdlife on the ley I hardly noticed the muted roar of traffic on the road. The wet wind on my back was OK but a brighter day might have produced more birds including the stonechats, reed buntings, Cetti's warblers and cirl buntings which are resident along with great crested grebes, water rails and herons.

Around this time of year, though, divers, grebes, all sorts of ducks from goldeneye to long-tailed and eider bitterns and goosanders can be seen if you're beady enough. But I was there for the total outdoor experience – weather, the freshwater lagoons, the bay, the sky and that keen sense of freedom beyond the clutter of houses.

Presently I was beside Slapton Ley with Hartshorn Plantation across the water, France Wood beyond, and the inlet of Ireland Bay below a green hillside which concealed the village of Slapton. You can walk the Nature Trail the landward end of the little bridge and follow the edge of Ireland Bay to the wetland before cutting up into Slapton Village. Cross the bridge and the trail begins at the gate on the left.

Marching beside the reed-choked Higher Ley to the tangle of reeds and scrub willow of the Gara Valley, I kept my eyes open for wildlife. And sure enough,

grazing in a field overlooking the wetland was a big flock of Canada geese.

At Strete Gate and the bend I crossed the road and turned to come back along the top of the shore. Beach walking isn't easy here. The gritty sand "gives" underfoot and I prefer the rough turf close to the road. Anyway, the rain decided to stop and I just had the south west wind on my face and the remarkable seascape for my return to Torcross.

The beach falls steeply to the waves and anglers were trying their luck along the tideline. Behind the dark profile of Torcross Point the coast curved to Start Point, but the wind was in the wrong direction or I would have had one of the bay's awesome surf displays.

Walking past the Memorial erected by the US government to the people of the South Hams who sacrificed so much during the build up to D-Day I came on along the sandy path with fine views of the leys and Torcross waiting at the end of the trail.

One of the really attractive aspects of the walk is the vastness of Start Bay and the sky above it. The beach, the leys and the farmland beyond contribute to the quality of the walk. There's a Hebridean texture about it all that makes noisier and more popular seaside tourist areas seem claustrophobic in comparison. But

beauty apart, if you want to blow the festive season cobwebs from your mind or shed the faint muzziness of a hangover this shoreline stroll is just what the doctor ordered.

By now I had reached the door of The Start Bay Inn, and before long I had a glass of Luscombe's cider in my hand. All I fancied to eat was a bowl of chips but if you enjoy good food there's plenty on offer in this thatched pub. The sea food is a speciality and the bar is never empty. It has an open fire and two No Smoking areas. Catering for families is one of landlord Paul Stubbs' priorities, and apart from the cuisine there's a jukebox and a pool table. But the emphasis is on wining and dining (or lunching).

Paul Stubbs joined me in the snug of the top bar where a mix of generations had gathered to do justice to Sunday lunch. He's owned and run The Start Bay Inn since 1978.

"I employ three chefs," he said. "And quite a lot of the seafood they cook I catch. The rest comes from trawlers fishing in the bay."

Throughout the summer the landlord, who is definitely not a landlubber, dives for scallops or uses his rod and line to haul in bass and other shore-hugging delicacies. No wonder fish dishes dominate a comprehensive menu.

I was more interested in the "agricultural wine" – the ciders, and you have a choice of three at The Start Bay Inn. Addlestone, Copperhead and the luscious Luscombe's which is an aristocrat among farm ciders and has the dark autumnal flavour of apples through and through.

Picking away at my chips I saw off the cider and wondered if I could find room for a brace of smoked mackerel. In the end I decided to concentrate on the Luscombes. With a lift home it would have been stupid to have wasted an opportunity to do justice to the sort of Windfall Wine my old Dad would have killed for.

OTHER TITLES FROM OBELISK PUBLICATIONS